Hello!
I am a snake.

I0115152

Snakes are reptiles.

Nice to meet you.

I am all over the world.

Snakes can be found on every continent except Antarctica.

Snakes can live in various habitats like the desert...

I like it hot.

...or snakes can live in the forest.

My favorite color is green.

Snakes "hibernate" in colder weather to stay warm.

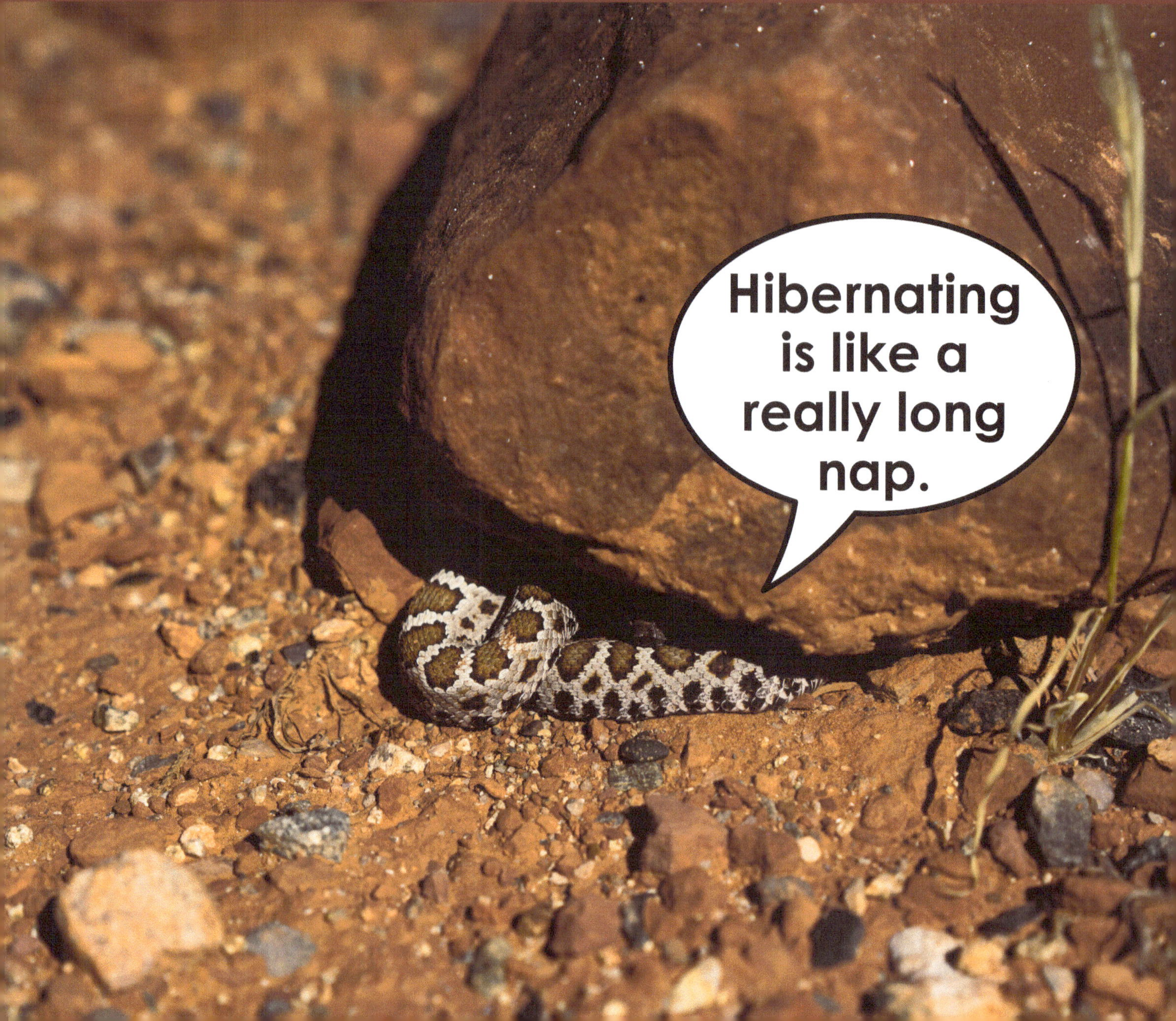

Snakes can make homes in all sorts of places like high in trees or under a rock.

Snakes are cold-blooded.

I'm a cold-blooded snake!

That means their body temperature depends on their environment.

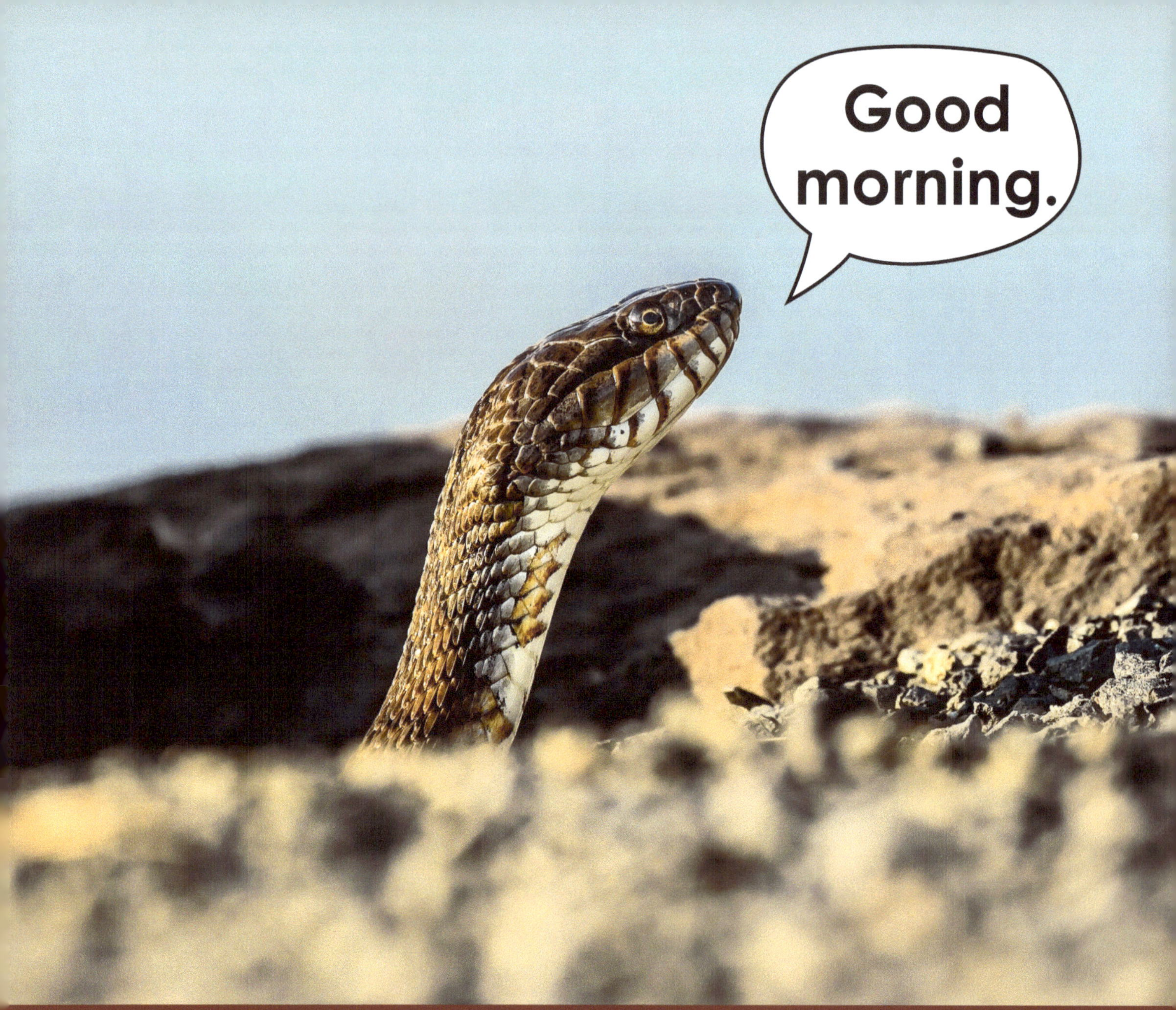

Snakes can be active during the day, which is called “diurnal”...

...or at night, which means snakes can be "nocturnal".

A group of snakes is typically called a "den" or a "bed."

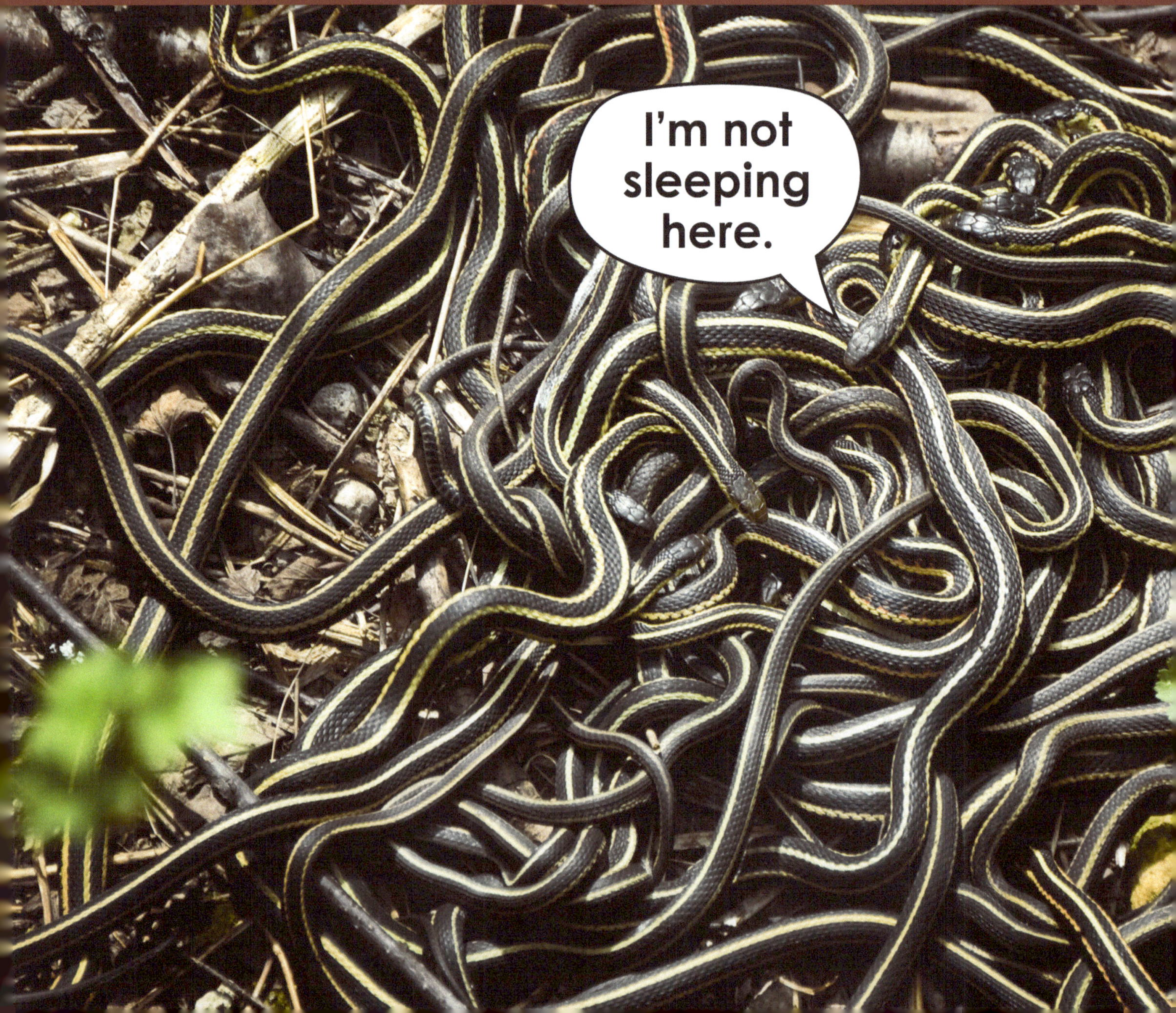

But, most snakes like to be alone and do not spend time with other snakes.

Snakes blend in to hide from predators and sneak up on prey.

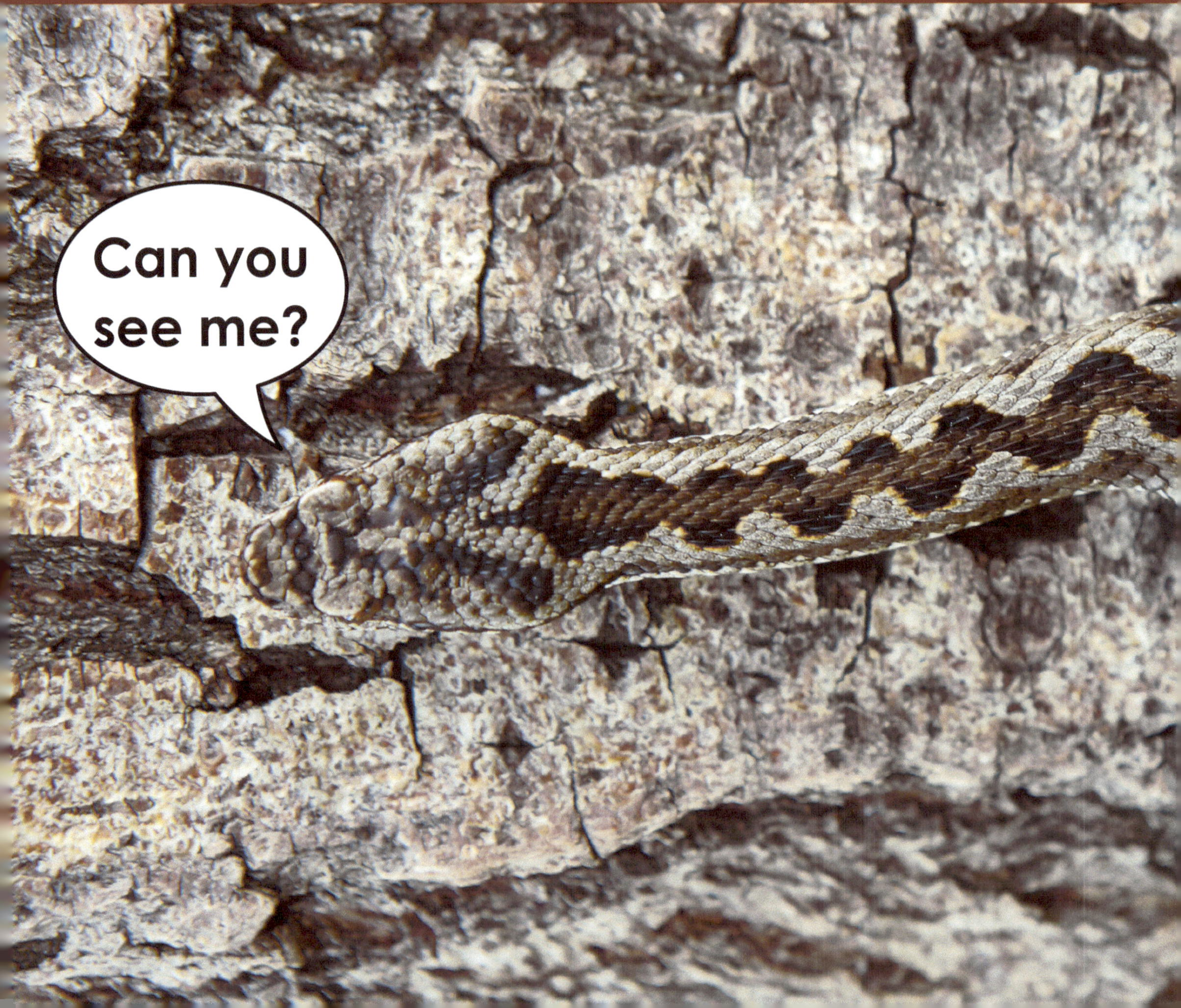

Snakes come in all different colors and patterns.

Snakes shed their skin as they grow.

Change is good.

Snakes have scales all over their bodies, and these scales help protect them.

My scales are cool and smooth.

They use their tongues to smell the air.

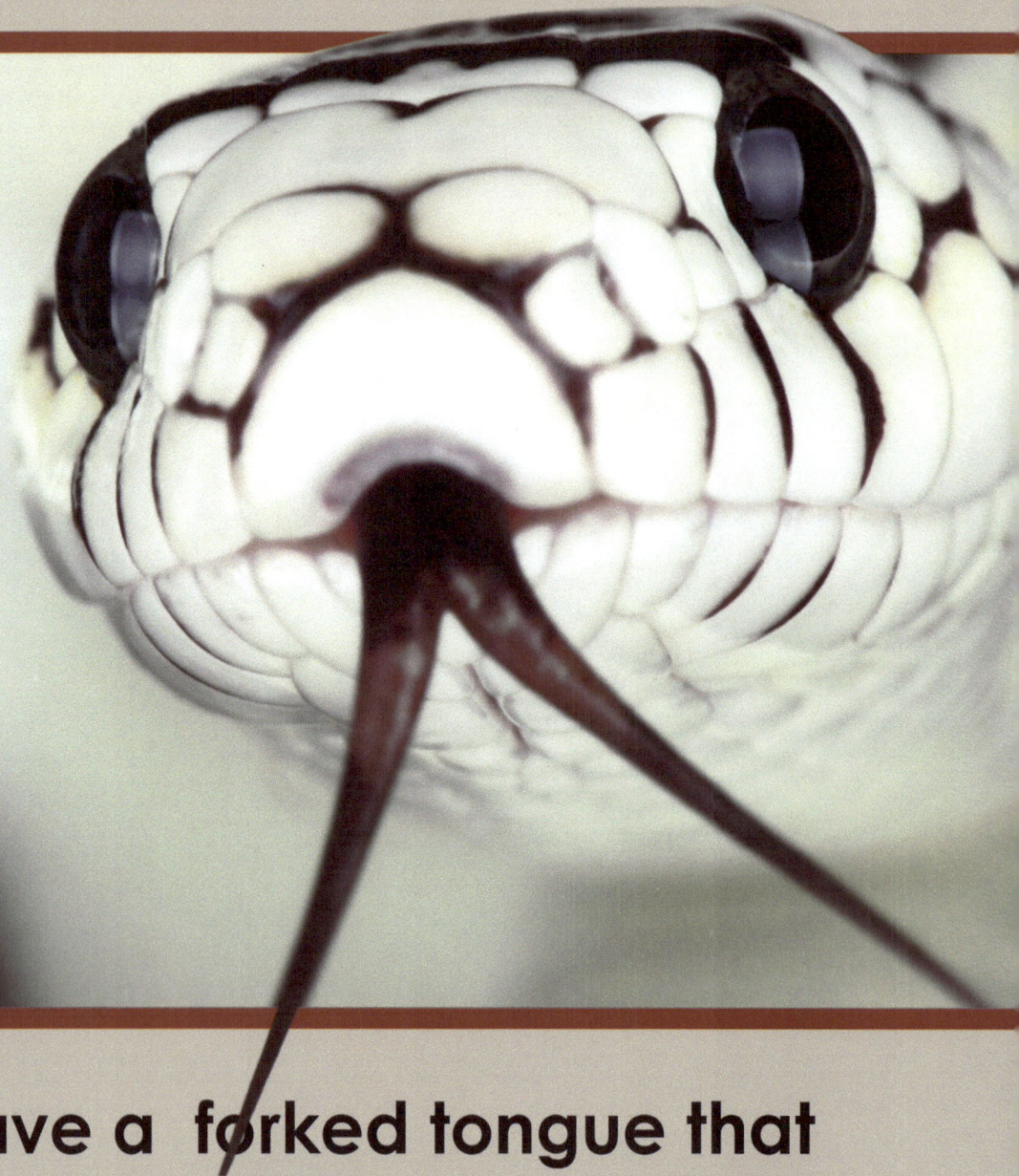

Snakes have a forked tongue that helps them sense their surroundings.

Snakes can eat animals like mice, birds, and insects.

I am important to the world because I help take care of pests!

Some snakes are "venomous", which means they have poison.

Red and black, friend of Jack; red and yellow, kills a fellow.

Snakes are unique because they lay eggs and leave them in a warm safe place.

Baby snakes are called "snakelets" or "hatchlings".

Where did mom go?

Snakelets are usually on their own from the moment they hatch.

Talk about growing up fast!

Snakelets are born with venom, but it's not as strong as adult snakes'.

Some snakes make a rattling noise with their tail, like the rattlesnake.

I'm warning you!

Snakes are known for their hissing sounds.

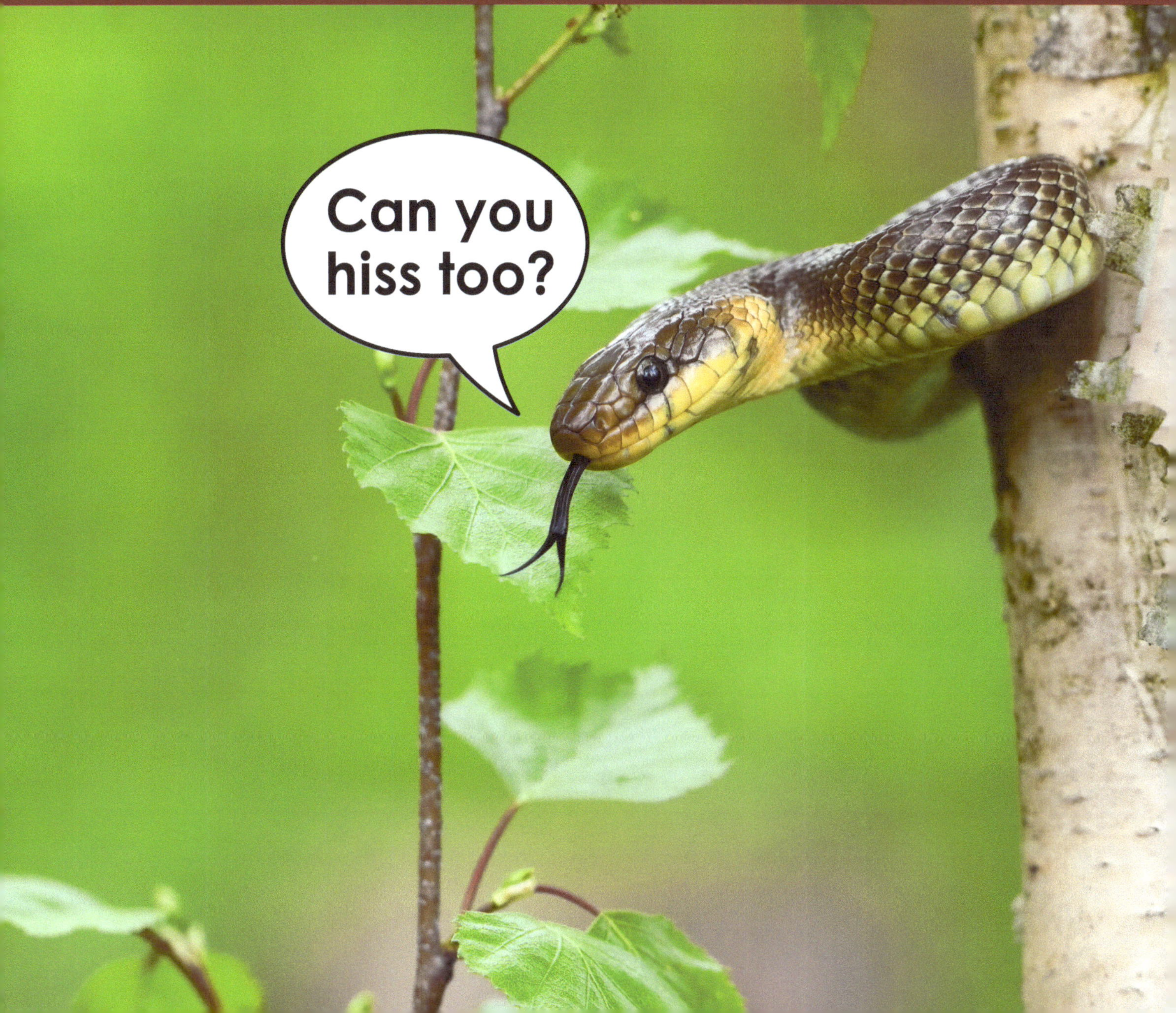

Some snakes are great swimmers
and can move through water easily.

Not all snakes are dangerous, and most are harmless to humans.

Stay back!

IT'S IMPORTANT TO ADMIRE SNAKES FROM A SAFE DISTANCE AND DO NOT DISTURB THEM IN THE WILD.

Hello parents!

Visit us to find out about new releases and **FREE** offers. We'll let you know when we have a new release coming out and how you can get it for FREE.

And you can cast your vote for what book we make next!

scan here

or visit here

ActiveBrainsBooks.com

---

scan here

Let us know what you think. As an independent publisher, your honest reviews mean a lot to us and our business. We'd love to hear from you!

amazon.com/review/create-review/

or visit here

FOLLOW US on Amazon.

amazon.com/author/activebrainsbooks

ACTIVE BRAINS

ActiveBrainsBooks.com